HOLIDAY
Parties

Let's Throw a St. Patrick's Day Party!

Rachel Lynette

PowerKiDS press.

New York

Published in 2012 by The Rosen Publishing Group, Inc.
29 East 21st Street, New York, NY 10010

First Edition

Editor: Joanne Randolph
Layout Design: Greg Tucker

Photo Credits: Cover (main), p.16 BananaStock/Thinkstock; cover (inset), pp. 10, 12 iStockphoto/Thinkstock; p. 4 © www.iStockphoto.com/Liza McCorkle; p. 5 Jupiterimages/Comstock/Thinkstock; p. 6 3LH-Fine Art/Getty Images; pp. 7, 8, 11, 14, 17 (left), 20–21 Shutterstock.com; p. 9 © www.iStockphoto.com/Donna Coleman; pp. 10–11 © www.iStockphoto.com/pixhook; p. 13 Jupiterimages/Photos.com/Thinkstock; p. 15 Burke/Triolo Productions/Getty Images; p. 17 (right) © www.iStockphoto.com/Jack Puccio; p. 22 © www.iStockphoto.com/Cathleen Clapper.

Library of Congress Cataloging-in-Publication Data

Lynette, Rachel.
  Let's throw a St. Patrick's Day party! / by Rachel Lynette. — 1st ed.
     p. cm. — (Holiday parties)   DEC 2 1 2011
  Includes index.
  ISBN 978-1-4488-2574-5 (library binding) — ISBN 978-1-4488-2737-4 (pbk.) —
ISBN 978-1-4488-2738-1 (6-pack)
  1. Saint Patrick's Day decorations—Juvenile literature. 2. Saint Patrick's Day—Juvenile literature.
3. Cooking, Irish—Juvenile literature. 4. Children's parties—Juvenile literature. I. Title.
  TT900.S25L96 2012
  745.594'162—dc22
                                              2010034283

Manufactured in the United States of America

CPSIA Compliance Information: Batch #WW11PK: For Further Information contact Rosen Publishing, New York, New York at 1-800-237-9932

Contents

Wear Your Green!

March 17 is a special day. It is the day we **celebrate** St. Patrick's Day. St. Patrick's Day is a time to celebrate Irish **culture**. You do not have to be Irish to celebrate, though. On St. Patrick's Day, people wear green. They look for **shamrocks** and try to catch **leprechauns**.

On St. Patrick's Day, people wear green and celebrate Irish culture and history. This boy wears a headband with shamrocks, which are an Irish symbol, on it.

St. Patrick's Day is also a time for parties! Maybe you have had a St. Patrick's Day party at school. School parties are fun, but you can also throw a party at home. There are many yummy St. Patrick's Day treats you can serve and fun activities you can plan.

It Started with a Saint

Saint Patrick lived many years ago in the fifth century. He helped spread **Christianity** in Ireland. After he died, in the mid- to late 400s, he was made a saint. St. Patrick's Day began as a time to honor this important man.

Since the 1600s, people have worn something green on St. Patrick's Day. Green is a great color to honor Ireland. Emerald is a bright green color. Ireland's land is so green that it

Here Saint Patrick, in white, is talking to people about Christianity and God.

is sometimes called the Emerald Isle. The Irish flag also has green on it.

Many people wear shamrocks on their clothing on St. Patrick's Day, too. Shamrocks grow naturally all over Ireland and are a **symbol** of the country. Shamrocks are thought to bring good luck!

Every St. Patrick's Day, 40 pounds (18 kg) of green vegetable dye are added to the Chicago River, in Illinois. The dye turns the river green for several hours!

Party Planning

Are you ready to plan your party? It is a good idea to start planning about a month before the big day. Begin by making a list of everyone you would like to **invite**. Make sure to send your invitations out at least two weeks before your party.

Throwing a party is fun if you are organized. Being organized means you have everything well planned out. Lists are a great tool to make sure you remember everything you need to do and buy.

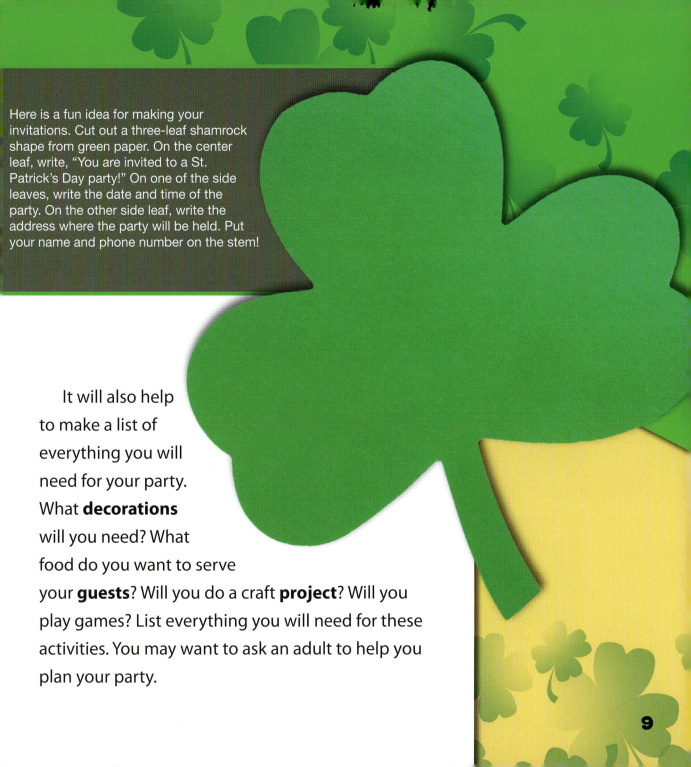

Here is a fun idea for making your invitations. Cut out a three-leaf shamrock shape from green paper. On the center leaf, write, "You are invited to a St. Patrick's Day party!" On one of the side leaves, write the date and time of the party. On the other side leaf, write the address where the party will be held. Put your name and phone number on the stem!

It will also help to make a list of everything you will need for your party. What **decorations** will you need? What food do you want to serve your **guests**? Will you do a craft **project**? Will you play games? List everything you will need for these activities. You may want to ask an adult to help you plan your party.

St. Patrick's Day Party Decorations

How will you decorate for your party? Of course, you will want to use a lot of green in your decorations. You can use green streamers and balloons. You can hang a string of green lights. There are also many decorations you can make.

Top: Shamrock cutouts can be taped to walls and windows or hung from the ceiling. *Right*: Make shamrock balloons to decorate your home. Just blow up three green balloons and tie them together with green curling ribbon, as shown.

You can make or buy green shamrock garlands to hang around the room. A paper leprechaun hat can make a good centerpiece on the table, too.

Use green construction paper to make cutouts of shamrocks and leprechaun hats. You can put them on the walls, or tie them to strings and hang them from the ceiling. You could use green or black construction paper to make a pot for leprechaun gold. Make the gold from circles of yellow paper. Then glue them to the top of the pot.

A Table Fit for a Leprechaun

Start by setting your table with a green tablecloth. Use green plates, cups, and napkins if you can. You can also decorate cups with St. Patrick's Day stickers. You can make napkin rings by cutting empty paper-towel tubes into 1-inch (2.5 cm) pieces. Paint each piece green. Then glue a paper shamrock to the top.

Put shiny green shamrocks on a big paper or glass plate. Then put a smaller plate on top. If you want to add a nice extra touch, put a small plastic leprechaun hat on top of each place setting.

You can use science to make a centerpiece. You will need to start this project a few days before your party. Fill a vase with water and add plenty of green food coloring. Then put some white daisies or carnations in the vase. Over the next few days, the flowers will take in the water and turn the petals green!

Do you want to try something fun? Draw and cut out several small leprechauns. You could also print them out from the computer. Hide them around the table. For example, you could hide one under a plate with just the hat sticking out. You could put one between the folds of a napkin, too. Your guests will have fun finding all the leprechauns!

What's Cooking?

It is fun to serve green food on St. Patrick's Day! You can use cookie cutters to make sugar cookies in St. Patrick's Day shapes, such as shamrocks and leprechaun hats. Then you can frost the cookies with green icing.

For another fun snack, try mixing a few drops of green food coloring into whipped cream

You can make cupcakes for your St. Patrick's Day party. Just frost them with green icing. You will have a snack fit for a leprechaun!

Use the same green icing to frost sugar cookies in fun St. Patrick's Day shapes. Try cutting some in the shape of shamrocks, hats, and pots of gold.

cheese. Spread the green cream cheese onto celery sticks. Place several golden raisins on top to look like pieces of leprechaun's gold.

You can also make leprechaun punch for your guests. Just pour a large bottle of lemon-lime soda into a punch bowl. Then add a carton of lime sherbet. As the sherbet melts, it will turn the punch green!

15

Irish Soda Bread

People in Ireland first started making soda bread in the 1800s. Most people did not have ovens then. They baked the bread in large cast-iron pots that they put right on the fire. Today, people often serve Irish soda bread on St. Patrick's Day. Because this is a baking project, you will need an adult to help you.

What you need:

4 cups all-purpose flour
1 teaspoon salt
2 tablespoons sugar
1 teaspoon baking soda
2 cups buttermilk
½ cup softened butter
2 cups raisins (optional)

What you do:

1

Preheat the oven to 425 degrees. Then grease and flour a round cake pan.

2

Mix the flour, salt, sugar, and baking soda in a large bowl.

3

Make a well in the center, and add the softened butter and the buttermilk. After the batter is well mixed, stir in the raisins if you are using them.

4

Mix it all together. Try not to mix it for over 1 minute.

5

Put the dough into the cake pan. Use a knife to cut a large cross on the top. Bake at 425 degrees for 40 minutes.

6

Cut the bread into pieces to serve. Irish soda bread is yummy with butter and jam!

Make a Leprechaun Hat

What you need:

Green poster board
Green construction paper
Black construction paper
Yellow construction paper
Scissors
Glue
Tape

What you do:

1

Cut a long strip of poster board to make a headband.

2

Draw a hat shape on a piece of green construction paper, and cut it out.

3

Cut a strip of black construction paper for the hatband. Glue it to the hat, just above the brim. Cut off the extra black paper on the edges.

4

Cut a buckle out of yellow construction paper, and glue it to the hatband.

5

Tape the hat to the headband. The headband should be a little bit above the bottom of the hat, as shown.

6

Ask an adult to tape or staple the headband so that it fits around your head.

19

Leprechaun Games

You can play leprechaun freeze tag. To play, the person who is it is the human. The other guests are the leprechauns. You can even have the leprechauns wear their leprechaun hats!

When the human tags a leprechaun, the leprechaun is frozen until another leprechaun tags her.

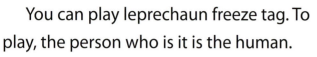

You can have your leprechauns race for the pot of gold. Set up a finish line, line up your guests, and run!

You can also have a gold coin toss. Place a large pot on a stool or chair. Use string to make a line several feet (m) away from the pot. Let each guest stand behind the line and try to toss chocolate gold coins into the pot. You can let your guests eat the coins that make it into the pot!

Find the Pot of Gold

You can send your guests on a treasure hunt to find the leprechaun's pot of gold! If you want to have a treasure hunt, you will need to plan ahead. Ask an adult to help you.

You can make a pot of gold to use at the end of your treasure hunt by asking an adult to help you paint a clean flowerpot black. When it is dry, fill it with chocolate coins or other prizes.

During the treasure hunt, your guests will work as a team to find clues. Each clue will bring them closer to the treasure. For example, the first clue could say, "Brrrrr, it's cold in here!" That would lead your guests to the refrigerator, where the second clue is hidden. Your guests will find the clues one by one, until they reach the pot of gold at the end of the hunt!

Glossary

celebrate (SEH-luh-brayt) To honor an important moment by doing special things.

Christianity (kris-chee-A-nih-tee) A faith based on the teachings of Jesus Christ and the Bible.

culture (KUL-chur) The beliefs, practices, and arts of a group of people.

decorations (deh-kuh-RAY-shunz) Things that make something prettier.

guests (GESTS) People invited to a party.

invite (in-VYT) To ask people if they will come to a party.

leprechauns (LEP-ruh-konz) Elves from Irish fairy tales.

project (PRAH-jekt) A special job that someone does.

saint (SAYNT) A person who is honored by the Christian church for leading a holy life.

shamrocks (SHAM-roks) Clovers with three leaflets.

symbol (SIM-bul) An object or a picture that stands for something else.

Index

Web Sites

Due to the changing nature of Internet links, PowerKids Press has developed an online list of Web sites related to the subject of this book. This site is updated regularly. Please use this link to access the list:
www.powerkidslinks.com/hp/stpat/